HOW TO HEAR FROM GOD
everyday

A guide on more than
30 ways God communicates to us

Bishop Dr. Joseph C. Kanu

© 2022 Bishop (Dr.) Joseph C. Kanu

All right reserved: No part of this publication may be reproduced, retrieved or stored in any retrieval system; electronically, mechanical or otherwise without the written permission of the author and the publisher.

Unless otherwise indicated, all scripture quotations are taken from the King James Version of the Bible.

ISBN: 978-1-100-21764-2

Book cover design and Printing by
tmacre8tv@gmail.com
(+2348137371249)

Formatted by Framedwordsintl
(+2348139410461)

How To Hear From God Everyday

Contents

ACKNOWLEDGMENT 7
DEDICATION 8
FOREWORD 9
CHAPTER ONE 10
Preparation for his voice 10
Introduction 10
Before we hear God's voice 10
The Lord Calls Samuel 11
The voice of God 13
Ways of preparation 14
Get water baptized: 18
Get baptized by the Holy Spirit 21
Draw closer to God: 23
How to draw closer to God 25
By church fellowship 27
CHAPTER TWO 29
The ways that God speaks and communicates to us 29
Introduction 29
How God speaks 29

How To Hear From God Everyday

Voice - Still small voice: 30
The Word/Bible 32
Inner witness 34
Dreams 36
Visions 44
Trance 49
Nature/Creation/Animals/Things 51
Impressions 56
Confirmations 60
Prophets 62
Testimony 4 64
Testimony 5 64
Experiences/Circumstances 65
People 66
Knowing that you know 66
Urim and Thummim 69
Revelations and Rhema 71
Votes - casting of lots 72
Tests: 74
Signs and wonders 76
Interpretations 77
Symbols 79

How To Hear From God Everyday

Messengers/Angels 81

Hebrews 13:2 85

Men and Women of God 85

Pictures 86

Promptings and feelings 88

The Holy Spirit 89

Messages: 90

Journalism/ Journaling 93

Translations 94

Testimonies 98

Thoughts 100

Patterns and Repetition 101

Inspiration 103

Exercising Your senses 104

TEN Hindrances to hearing God's voice and how to overcome them 108

CHAPTER THREE 124

How to know God's permissive and perfect will 124

Introduction 124

What is the will of God? 124

It is permissive and perfect 128

His will for us 133

How To Hear From God Everyday

CHAPTER FOUR	140
Hearing God's voice/choice	140
Introduction	140
His choice over our lives	144
CHAPTER FIVE	147
Impartation	147
Introduction	147
What is impartation?	147
Divine impartation	149
Its spiritual importance	154
Thy will be done	158
Reference list	160
Altar call to receive Christ	162
Prayer Points	164
About the Author	169
Contact Details	173

ACKNOWLEDGMENT

I wrote this book with the inspiration of the Holy Spirit and I want to give thanks to God for granting me the grace to write.

I also wish to use this opportunity to bless our Father in Heaven for His divine grace that eradicates shame and reproach and for how far He has brought me in a short while.

DEDICATION

I want to dedicate this book to The Holy Spirit because He is my source. To my parents, siblings, family, children, mother in love, especially my wife who works behind the scenes for the success of our family and ministry. To my spiritual father, church family, spiritual sons and daughters. I love you all.

FOREWORD

This book is in direct accordance with the message given to me by God. I personally wrote it down as a sermon and an educational prophetic book. The purpose of this spiritual message is to critically and elaborately shed light on the ways God speaks to us and how we can hear from Him.

Hearing from God gives us a sense of peace or joy that engulfs our body in a moment of chaos. It gives life to the lifeless and hope to the hopeless. So I pray that the Lord almighty in His infinite mercy bestows upon you, joy and peace of the mind, body and spirit along with riches and glory in Jesus name, Amen.

CHAPTER ONE

Preparation for his voice

Introduction

We shall begin by discussing in this chapter, what God's voice is, what needs to be done before we hear it, and ways of preparing to hear God's voice. Be blessed as you begin this spiritually enlightening book in the mighty name of Jesus. Amen.

Before we hear God's voice

There are several teachings and books on how to hear the voice of God. However, this book offers you an opportunity to prepare to not just hear but identify the voice of God.

How To Hear From God Everyday

When Samuel first heard the voice of God calling him, he thought it was the voice of his master Prophet Eli calling him.

1 Samuel 3:1-11

The Lord Calls Samuel

(1) And the child Samuel ministered unto the LORD before Eli. And the word of the LORD was precious in those days; *there was* no open vision.

(2) And it came to pass at that time, when Eli *was* laid down in his place, and his eyes began to wax dim, *that* he could not see;

(3) And ere the lamp of God went out in the temple of the LORD, where the ark of God *was*, and Samuel was laid down *to sleep*;

(4) That the LORD called Samuel: and he answered, Here *am* I.

(5) And he ran unto Eli, and said, Here *am* I; for thou calledst me. And he said, I called not; lie down again. And he went and lay down.

(6) And the LORD called yet again, Samuel. And Samuel arose and went to Eli, and said, Here *am* I; for thou didst call me. And he answered, I called not, my son; lie down again.

(7) Now Samuel did not yet know the LORD, neither was the word of the LORD yet revealed unto him.

(8) And the LORD called Samuel again the third time. And he arose and went to Eli, and said, Here *am* I; for thou didst call me. And Eli perceived that the LORD had called the child.

(9) Therefore, Eli said unto Samuel, Go, lie down: and it shall be, if he call thee, that thou shalt say, Speak, LORD; for thy servant heareth. So Samuel went and lay down in his place.

God's Judgment against Eli

(10) And the LORD came, and stood, and called as at other times, Samuel, Samuel. Then Samuel answered, Speak; for thy servant heareth.

(11) And the LORD said to Samuel, Behold, I will do a thing in Israel, at which both the ears of every one that heareth it shall tingle

The voice of God

So what is the voice of God? We shall first identify God (all of Him), in three parts. GOD is a Consciousness, a Body, and a Voice.

The consciousness is the Father, Jesus Christ is the body, and the Holy Spirit is the voice. The Father is the instructor, Jesus is our proof that the instructions of the Father are applicable to us, and the Holy Spirit is the deliverer of the instructions.

> **The voice of God is the Holy Spirit.**

God spoke to Apostle peter through his spirit. This is how the Bible puts it in Acts 10:19 While Peter thought about the vision, the Spirit said to him, "Behold, three men are seeking you.it was the spirit that said to him... emphasis added.

Ways of preparation

God our Father is with us all the time. However, we don't know when God will speak to us directly, so we should prepare to have a heart that's ready to listen to Him at any time. There are five major actions we must take in order to hear from God, these are enumerated below:

1. Becoming God's sheep by becoming born again:

References to sheep are found throughout the Bible. Sheep were often used as sacrificial animals in the Old Testament. Furthermore, they were also a primary source of income in ancient Middle Eastern cultures. But sheep in this context, are used symbolically to represent God's people and to be of God, we must be born again. The Bible even refers to Jesus Christ as the "Lamb of God".

John 10:3, 27 KJV (3)To him the porter openeth; and the sheep hear his voice: and he calleth his own sheep by name, and leadeth them out.

(27) My sheep hear my voice, and I know them, and they follow me:

To hear God's voice, we must belong to God. Jesus said, "My sheep listen to my voice; I know them, and they follow me" (John 10:27). Those who hear God's voice are those who belong to Him—those who have been saved by His grace through faith in the Lord Jesus. These are the sheep who hear and recognize His voice, because they know Him as their Shepherd. If we are to recognize God's voice, we must belong to Him.

Though there could be exemptions where God drastically intervenes in people's life to speak to them without them being born again because He has a special reason or assignment.

In such cases, those people did not prepare to hear His voice, God decided to speak to them. Like in the case of Saul the slayer who later became Paul the preacher after God spoke to him.

How To Hear From God Everyday

Acts 9:3-9

King James Version

³ And as he journeyed, he came near Damascus: and suddenly there shined round about him a light from heaven:

⁴ And he fell to the earth, and heard a voice saying unto him, Saul, Saul, why persecutest thou me?

⁵ And he said, Who art thou, Lord? And the Lord said, I am Jesus whom thou persecutest: it is hard for thee to kick against the pricks.

⁶ And he trembling and astonished said, Lord, what wilt thou have me to do? And the Lord said unto him, Arise, and go into the city, and it shall be told thee what thou must do.

2

Get water baptized: Water baptism signifies the believer's total trust in and total reliance on the Lord Jesus Christ, as well as a commitment to live obediently to Him. It also expresses unity with all the saints, that is, with every person in every nation on earth who is a member of the Body of Christ. Water baptism conveys this and many more. We are saved by grace through faith.

Matthew 28:19 KJV Go ye therefore, and teach all nations, baptizing them in the name of the Father, and of the Son, and of the Holy Ghost:

Moreover, water baptism is for believers. Before we are baptized, we must come to believe that we are sinners in need of salvation. We must also believe that Christ died on the cross to pay for our sins, that He was buried, and that He was resurrected to assure our place in heaven. So water baptism signifies the death, burial and resurrection of Jesus Christ. It also signifies divine recognition as evidenced in Matthew 3: 13-17:

Matthew 3:13-17 KJV Then cometh Jesus from Galilee to Jordan unto John, to be baptized of him.

(14) But John forbad him, saying, I have need to be baptized of thee, and comest thou to me?

(15) And Jesus answering said unto him, Suffer it to be so now: for thus it becometh us to fulfil all righteousness. Then he suffered him.

(16) And Jesus, when he was baptized, went up straightway out of the water: and, lo, the heavens were opened unto him, and he saw the Spirit of God descending like a dove, and lighting upon him:

How To Hear From God Everyday

(17) And lo a voice from heaven, saying, This is my beloved Son, in whom I am well pleased.

Verse 17 says that there was a voice from heaven that spoke when Jesus got baptized. By getting water baptized, we not only obey Christ's command but are following in His footsteps and having faith that what happened to Jesus will start happening to us, That is, The voice of God will start speaking t us from the day we get baptised.

And if you have been baptised already, you can ask God to start speaking to you right now as He did to Christ when He was baptised.

3

Get baptized by the Holy Spirit:

The baptism of the Holy Spirit may be defined as an act whereby the Spirit of God positions the believer into union with Christ and into union with other believers in the body of Christ at the moment of salvation. The baptism of the Holy Spirit was first predicted by John the Baptist in Mark 1:8, and by Jesus in Acts 1:5 which reads:

Mark 1:8 KJV I indeed have baptized you with water: but he shall baptize you with the Holy Ghost.

Acts 1:5 For John truly baptized with water; but ye shall be baptized with the Holy Ghost not many days hence.

In the book of Acts, just before Jesus ascended to Heaven, He told the disciples that the Holy Ghost would come. He instructed them to tarry in

Jerusalem until they received the "promise of the Father," which was the Holy Spirit. The scriptures tells us that a group of 120 people gathered in an upper room in the city of Jerusalem, and they prayed. They had gathered there with a single purpose in mind: the Lord had promised He would send power upon them and they were determined to receive it.

Acts 1:8 KJV But ye shall receive power, after that the Holy Ghost is come upon you: and ye shall be witnesses unto me both in Jerusalem, and in all Judaea, and in Samaria, and unto the uttermost part of the earth.

Furthermore, the scripture tells us that something occurred in that upper room that they had never witnessed or experienced before—the power of God descended upon them and they were filled with the Holy Spirit.

> *Since the Holy spirit is the voice of God, when you receive The Holy Spirit, you receive God's voice!*

That's why it is important as you prepare to hear God's voice, you must pray, fast, seek laying on of hands, be baptised with the Holy Spirit. And if you have already, pray and ask Him to start speaking to you in a language you will understand.

4

Draw closer to God: *The phrase, "draw near," means, very simply, to approach or get close to a thing. To draw near to God, means then, to get close to God. If you get close to God, James is saying, God Himself will come to be close to you.*

Furthermore, the Bible tells us in James 4:8, that:

James 4:8 KJV Draw nigh to God, and he will draw nigh to you. Cleanse your hands, ye sinners; and purify your hearts, ye double minded.

Look at it this way; when you say you are close to someone, it means you have a relationship and you communicate. You become so close that you even have an unspoken understanding between you. Even if you are put together with one thousand other people and you were all to be blind folded, you will still be able to identify each of them when you hear their voices, you will say, I know that voice, But why would you say that? simply because you are close and over time have mastered each other's voices that you can recognise it anywhere. This is what has helped me recognise God's voice in my life. By drawing closer to God each day.

How to draw closer to God

1. Holiness: By living holy

Literally, holy living means that **the Christian lives a life that is set apart, reserved to give glory to God.** *It is a life of discipline, focus, and attention to matters of righteous living.*

Look at the scripture below

Hebrews 12:4 Follow peace with all men, and holiness, without which no man shall see the Lord:

> **So do you want to see God speak to you? live Holy. Holiness attracts God's attention to you.**

2. Watching, listening to and reading the Word

We are a product of what we watch, listen to and read. So when you keep watching, listening to and Godly programmes, talks and books, it helps to draw you closer to the things of God. I am a big fan of The Supernatural tv show run by Sid Roth. I learnt a lot about the supernatural from his shows and it helped draw me closer to God. Especially the testimonies, they will make you want more of God.

Romans 10:17

So then faith cometh by hearing, and hearing by the word of God.

When you watch a sermon, you hear God's word. When you listen to a Sermon, you hear God's word. When you read God's word, you hear His words with the ears of your mind and spirit and God speaks to you through rhema and revelation especially when particular scriptures jump out on you. As you continuously watch, listen and read, faith comes because you are hearing God's word.

3.

By church fellowship

Having constant fellowship with other believers can help draw you closer to God especially when we are dedicated to worshiping God. We get together to praise, pray, worship, fast, give, encourage and share testimonies. When you hear about the testimonies of people and how their closeness to God was a blessing to them, you would want to get even closer to God than ever before. This creates in us a desire and hunger to be closer to God.

So in conclusion to this chapter, we as Christians and believers can prepare to hear God's voice by first executing the four major actions that were enumerated above. I pray that the good Lord gives you the strength to see them through in the mighty name of Jesus. Amen.

CHAPTER TWO

The ways that God speaks and communicates to us

Introduction

Moving on, we shall now discuss the ways that God speaks and communicates to us. Furthermore, we shall shed light on God's way of calling us to fulfill our destiny and the coming of his kingdom.

How God speaks

People all over the world may be yearning to hear God's voice and probably ask questions within themselves like: "Is God speaking to us?" "Is it possible to hear His voice?"

"Does God want us to hear His voice?" "How does God speak?" "How are we to listen?".

Yes, God is speaking, and we can also hear His voice. Christianity is fundamentally a relationship, and every relationship is established and maintained through communication. It is essential that we Christians learn to hear God's voice, so that we may deepen our relationship with our heavenly Father. Below are several examples of how God speaks and communicates with us:

1.

Voice - Still small voice: There is only one place in the Scriptures where God is said to speak in a "still small voice," and it was to Elijah after his dramatic victory over the prophets of Baal in the book of 1 Kings. The point of God speaking in the still small voice was to show Elijah that the work of God need not always be accompanied by dramatic revelation or manifestations. So in essence, Divine silence does not necessarily mean divine inactivity.

1 Kings 19:11-13 KJV And he said, Go forth, and stand upon the mount before the LORD. And, behold, the LORD passed by, and a great and strong wind rent the mountains, and brake in pieces the rocks before the LORD; but the LORD was not in the wind: and after the wind an earthquake; but the LORD was not in the earthquake:

And after the earthquake a fire; but the LORD was not in the fire: and after the fire a <u>still small voice</u>.

And it was so, when Elijah heard it, that he wrapped his face in his mantle, and went out, and stood in the entrance of the cave. And, behold, there came a voice unto him, and said, What doest thou here, Elijah?

You can practice hearing the still small voice of God by going to a place that is very quiet or create such an environment around you, after praising and worshiping God intensely for as long as you can, then remain silent and ask God to speak to your heart or simply just talk to you.

You can put down this book and try it now. If it doesn't work the first time, keep trying but make sure you bring quality repentance to God and you hold no malice or unforgiveness towards anyone.

2.

The Word/Bible: The Bible is one of God's provisions to equip us to do His will. God's Word is alive; it is active in our lives. The Bible is an absolutely essential part of your walk with God, so you must not neglect His Word. It is one way that He speaks to you personally, powerfully—today. Furthermore, not only are we to have a growing relationship with the Lord through His Word, but we also should be ready to give an answer to others whenever necessary.

2 Timothy 3:16-17 KJV *All scripture is given by inspiration of God, and is profitable for doctrine, for reproof, for correction, for instruction in righteousness:*

(17) That the man of God may be perfect, thoroughly furnished unto all good works.

1 Peter 3:15-16 KJV But sanctify the Lord God in your hearts: and be ready always to give an answer to every man that asketh you a reason of the hope that is in you with meekness and fear:

(16) Having a good conscience; that, whereas they speak evil of you, as of evildoers, they may be ashamed that

falsely accuse your good conversation in Christ.

So, studying the word of God helps you to understand and recognize how God speaks. God can speak to you directly by giving you a word for your situation. Have you ever experienced a time when you needed to hear from God and you turned the scriptures and miraculously, that's your answer right there. Sometimes, when you study the word of God, it appears as though some words jumped out on you and suddenly you have a deeper, clearer understanding and knowledge. That is God speaking to you directly from and through his written word.

3.

Inner witness: When the Holy Spirit speaks to your spirit, you do not hear an audible voice. This is what people call "the inner witness". The voice of the Holy Spirit to your spirit creates a quiet assurance—a relaxed knowing about something. A great secret to identifying the inner witness is to eliminate other voices. Ensure that it is not your flesh that wants to do something by focusing on Christ. Make sure that it is not just a reasonable proposition.

There may be some good reason and some good feelings when the Spirit is leading you, but make sure it is not just that by praying and asking God to silence other voices so you can hear him clearly.

Romans 8:16 KJV The Spirit itself beareth witness with our spirit, that we are the children of God:

Romans 9:1 KJV I say the truth in Christ, I lie not, my conscience also bearing me witness in the Holy Ghost,

Luke 24:32 KJV And they said one to another, Did not our heart burn within us, while he talked with us by the way, and while he opened to us the scriptures?

4.

Dreams: The Lord still uses our dreams to speak truth into our lives. However, this is a subtopic that requires great discernment because not every dream is a vision from God.

God is most likely using our dreams to speak with us because we don't often spend quiet time in our days listening to his voice. So If you have a dream that you think is from God, your first step should be to pray for understanding. Moreover, the Bible tells us in Numbers 12:6, that before Christ, dreams were a common way for the Lord to speak to His servants.

Numbers 12:6 KJV And he said, Hear now my words: If there be a prophet among you, I the LORD will make myself known unto him in a vision, and will speak unto him in a dream.

How To Hear From God Everyday

God can speak to you in dreams using people, men of God, Angels or objects which have meanings.

When God was calling me into ministry, I had a lot of dreams about airplanes and buses. It was God telling me about international and local ministries.

In the dream, the vehicles, trains or planes represented ministry and the type of car or plane represented the type of ministry. Buses represent local, city or national ministries because buses can travel such distances. Trains represent the same but very busy ministry because people get in and out at every stop. Planes represent international ministry. The driver or pilot is often the pastor or leader, the passengers are the members, engine size represent capacity, power or level of anointing, the drivers mate represent an evangelist because he is the one calling for passengers or making announcements, the petrol, diesel, fuel or charge represent The Holy Spirit, the engine represents prayer. These are some of the elements that make up a ministry

So you see how a small dream can actually be a big dream.

When God spoke to King Pharaoh through a dream twice, it later became a big dream that saved his nation from seven years of famine.

Genesis 41:15-44

¹⁵ And Pharaoh said unto Joseph, I have dreamed a dream, and there is none that can interpret it: and I have heard say of thee, that thou canst understand a dream to interpret it.

¹⁶ And Joseph answered Pharaoh, saying, It is not in me: God shall give Pharaoh an answer of peace.

¹⁷ And Pharaoh said unto Joseph, In my dream, behold, I stood upon the bank of the river:

¹⁸ And, behold, there came up out of the river seven kine, fatfleshed and well favoured; and they fed in a meadow:

¹⁹ And, behold, seven other kine came up after them, poor and very ill favoured and leanfleshed, such as I never saw in all the land of Egypt for badness:

²⁰ And the lean and the ill favoured kine did eat up the first seven fat kine:

²¹ And when they had eaten them up, it could not be known that they had eaten them; but they were still ill favoured, as at the beginning. So I awoke.

²² And I saw in my dream, and, behold, seven ears came up in one stalk, full and good:

²³ And, behold, seven ears, withered, thin, and blasted with the east wind, sprung up after them:

²⁴ And the thin ears devoured the seven good ears: and I told this unto the magicians; but there was none that could declare it to me.

²⁵ And Joseph said unto Pharaoh, The dream of Pharaoh is one: God hath shewed Pharaoh what he is about to do.

²⁶ The seven good kine are seven years; and the seven good ears are seven years: the dream is one.

²⁷ And the seven thin and ill favoured kine that came up after them are seven years; and the seven empty ears blasted with the east wind shall be seven years of famine.

²⁸ This is the thing which I have spoken unto Pharaoh: What God is about to do he sheweth unto Pharaoh.

²⁹ Behold, there come seven years of great plenty throughout all the land of Egypt:

³⁰ And there shall arise after them seven years of famine; and all the plenty shall be forgotten in the land of Egypt; and the famine shall consume the land;

³¹ And the plenty shall not be known in the land by reason of that famine following; for it shall be very grievous.

³² And for that the dream was doubled unto Pharaoh twice; it is because the thing is established by God, and God will shortly bring it to pass.

³³ Now therefore let Pharaoh look out a man discreet and wise, and set him over the land of Egypt.

³⁴ Let Pharaoh do this, and let him appoint officers over the land, and take up the fifth part of the land of Egypt in the seven plenteous years.

[35] And let them gather all the food of those good years that come, and lay up corn under the hand of Pharaoh, and let them keep food in the cities.

[36] And that food shall be for store to the land against the seven years of famine, which shall be in the land of Egypt; that the land perish not through the famine.

[37] And the thing was good in the eyes of Pharaoh, and in the eyes of all his servants.

[38] And Pharaoh said unto his servants, Can we find such a one as this is, a man in whom the Spirit of God is?

[39] And Pharaoh said unto Joseph, Forasmuch as God hath shewed thee all this, there is none so discreet and wise as thou art:

[40] Thou shalt be over my house, and according unto thy word shall all my

people be ruled: only in the throne will I be greater than thou.

⁴¹ And Pharaoh said unto Joseph, See, I have set thee over all the land of Egypt.

⁴² And Pharaoh took off his ring from his hand, and put it upon Joseph's hand, and arrayed him in vestures of fine linen, and put a gold chain about his neck;

⁴³ And he made him to ride in the second chariot which he had; and they cried before him, Bow the knee: and he made him ruler over all the land of Egypt.

⁴⁴ And Pharaoh said unto Joseph, I am Pharaoh, and without thee shall no man lift up his hand or foot in all the land of Egypt

If you don't dream or you simply can't remember your dreams, pray this prayer now while laying one hand over your head and one hand over your eyes.

My father my maker, I thank you for the gift of dreams. Now in the mighty name of Jesus Christ, whatever causes me not to dream or to forget my dreams, I command them to seize now.

I bind every spirit attacking my dream life

From today, I begin to dream Godly dreams and I will also remember them.

Repeat this prayer with passion and faith seven times.

Now put a pen and paper beside your bed and go to sleep.

You will wake up with a testimony.

5.

Visions: Visions mean "waking dreams". God uses visions to reveal His plans to His children. In the visions the Lord may reveal a message of encouragement or warning. The mercy of God is shown by the fact that He strengthens the weak and does not bring judgments upon men until He first warns them. However, It should be noted that not all visions are from the Lord. So, how do we know whether a vision is from God or not? The prophet Isaiah gives us the answer in Isaiah 8:20 which reads:

Isaiah 8:20 KJV *To the law and to the testimony: if they speak not according to this word, it is because there is no light in them.*

A good example of someone who God spoke to through a vision is Captain Cornelius.

Acts 10:1-6

10 There was a certain man in Caesarea called Cornelius, a centurion of the band called the Italian band,

² A devout man, and one that feared God with all his house, which gave much alms to the people, and prayed to God alway.

³ He saw in a vision evidently about the ninth hour of the day an angel of God coming in to him, and saying unto him, Cornelius.

⁴ And when he looked on him, he was afraid, and said, What is it, Lord? And he said unto him, Thy prayers and thine alms are come up for a memorial before God.

⁵ And now send men to Joppa, and call for one Simon, whose surname is Peter:

⁶ He lodgeth with one Simon a tanner, whose house is by the sea side: he shall tell thee what thou oughtest to do.

Acts 10:30-32

³⁰ And Cornelius said, Four days ago I was fasting until this hour; and at the ninth hour I prayed in my house, and, behold, a man stood before me in bright clothing,

³¹ And said, Cornelius, thy prayer is heard, and thine alms are had in remembrance in the sight of God.

³² Send therefore to Joppa, and call hither Simon, whose surname is Peter; he is lodged in the house of one Simon a tanner by the sea side: who, when he cometh, shall speak unto thee.

How To Hear From God Everyday

> **There are three keys here to use. Consistent prayers, for example giving yourself to prayers every day at particular times of the day, fasting and giving.**

These were they keys cornelius used. I use them and they work for me and they can work for you to.

See my book, prayers that availeth much on how to pray for an hour with ease and how to pray and fast for forty days.

At a point in my life and ministry, I was facing a lot of challenges so I began to pray and fast forty days. 5am to 12, 5am to 1pm, and sometimes till 3pm or more but my focus was on praying consistently every day from

5am before I went to work and from 10pm or 12 midnight.

It was a mixture of dry, water and daniels fast.

It opened up the heavens to me. It was one angelic encounter after the other including out of body experience when I was taken up like Ezekiel by Angels to the second heavens. I was so afraid, I begged the Angels to bring me down and they did.

In one of the encounters, I heard the Angels singing. Oh what a glorious symphony that words cannot describe.

And you can seek God for the same, just ask Him now.

6.

Trance:

God can speak through a trance (similar to a vision). A trance usually occurs in between sleep and being awake. So it catches up with you when you are about to fall asleep. So instead of falling asleep, you fall into a trance. Trance replaces or steps in between you and sleep

The Bible tells us that Peter fell into a trance while waiting for a meal to be prepared in Acts 10:10 which reads:

Acts 10:10 KJV *And he became very hungry, and would have eaten: but while they made ready, he fell into a trance,*

While in this trance he saw a vision focusing his heart on his need to minister to Gentiles. But why a trance? Some Christian scholars are uncertain why God spoke to Peter in this condition, but because of Peter's generational bias against Gentiles, it required three encounters with the heavenly voice while in the trance to persuade him. It's intriguing to also note that God used a trance in Peter's life to spread the gospel into the

Gentile world. Apparently, God believed that in this instance this was the best way to communicate with one of His servants.

This happens to me very often and sometimes the things I see are so terrifying that my reaction terrifies my wife all the time. Oh I feel sorry for her.

> **In my opinion, maintaining a lifestyle of consistent prayer, fellowship, commitment and communion with God goes a long way especially when you keep asking God to reveal things to you.**

7.

Nature/Creation/Animals/Things

From a historical standpoint, the concept of God speaking through creation is familiar to the Christian faith. One of the oldest creeds in the church, the Apostles' Creed, begins with the words that emphasize God's activity in creation: "We believe in God the Father Almighty, Maker of heaven and earth."

Jesus teaches us to look upon creation and listen as it declares to us the nature of God.

Nature reveals the glory of God. Nature teaches us more about God and His love for humanity. It shows us discipline, principle, law, fellowship, and love. Romans 1:20 sheds more light on this:

Romans 1:20 KJV For the invisible things of him from the creation of the world are clearly seen, being understood by the things that are made, even his eternal power and Godhead; so that they are without excuse:

Furthermore, Numbers 22 tells us the fascinating story of Balaam and his donkey. Balaam was on his way to help King Balak curse the Israelites, even though this displeased God. So God sent an angel to stand in Balaam's way. Balaam didn't see the angel, but his donkey did and refused to move. Balaam proceeded to beat the donkey thinking that she was just being stubborn, when finally a miracle happened in Numbers 22:28 KJV which reads:

And the LORD opened the mouth of the ass, and she said unto Balaam, What have I done unto thee, that thou hast smitten me these three times?

In this case, the donkey actually spoke. We may not have heard of any recent such occurrences but God has given animals such as pets heightened senses with which the speak to their owners. For example, there are guide dogs that lead the blind. They are so to say communicating with their owners and also able to show them the way. There are some dogs that are able to sense danger and warn their owners or even protect them or stop them from further harm like the donkey protected Balaam from being killed by the Angel, some dogs are able to detect epileptic fits before the start in their owners and are able to offer their owners protection.

Have you ever gone on prayer walks? And you notice something different about the areas which are familiar to you. This time, it may look or feel more peaceful or troublesome. In most cases, that's God speaking to you and it may be a response to your prayers. So pay particular attention to your feelings to see if they are peaceful or disturbed.

Talking about speaking through things, I remember an incident one day in 2012 when I was walking through the streets of London and I came to a particular street which I normally walk through before called Victoria St, but something happened which was different from the other times when I walked through, that name of the street Victoria St appeared to pop out from the sign and appeared to me but I didn't understand why so later on I saw this lady who was partially blind and I felt in my spirit to minister to her so as we sat on the bench by the bus stop in London talking I was ministering to her; the name of the street; Victoria, kept coming up in my mind as I was praying for her, I asked her: do you know anyone called Victoria? she said that's my daughter-in-law she's the one responsible for my illness so she went on to tell me everything Victoria did to her through witchcraft and all those things so just to tell you that God can speak to you through things so we began to pray for deliverance right on the street for to be set free in Jesus name, Amen.

8.

Impressions: An impression can be defined as an idea, feeling, or opinion about something or someone, especially one formed without conscious thought or on the basis of little evidence. So one of the ways God speaks is through impressions. When God speaks through impressions it can be described as an inner voice or God's still small voice. Hearing a "God planted thought" is one of the easiest and most common ways people hear from God.

One writer describes this as God thinking to us so you are not thinking about anything but suddenly this thought comes to you and this thought keeps coming to you and won't leave. It is not an imagination. This happens to me sometimes when I'm ministering and all my focus is on what I'm preaching. Then suddenly I see someone and this thought impressed me that I wasn't thinking about. I can stop and ask them a question just to confirm.

The thought impressed on me can even be the name of a person or place.

You can ask, does this name etc. make any meaning to you?

> *Another way that impressions can happen is when God wants to heal someone, God can impress what that person is feeling on you*

Testimony 1

I remember the first time I was preaching at The Redeemed Christian Church of God in Erith London as I was preaching I was feeling like I was having a heart attack and I know that I never had such symptoms before, I was in difficulty and pain and I was praying in my mind and preaching at the same time.

A voice like a thought, like when you remember the voice of someone or your mother talking to you. When you remember, she is not talking to you then but you remember it as though she is. That's how I remember hearing the voice and the instructions.

It said to me call it out, call out there's someone here and describe exactly what you're feeling as I did a midwife in the congregation came out and said she was the one having those symptoms

As I laid hands and prayed for her nothing seemed to happen but the following Sunday she came and gave testimony that the heart condition had stopped. She went to the hospital to check and got all clear. Sometimes I feel people's pain in my leg, my back or anywhere in my body that would normally be a mirror image or exactly where they're feeling those paints. Sometimes it can be pictures being impressed in your mind.

Testimony 2

I also remember one day I was ministering at Assemblies of God church in London Deptford. I was preaching and I had these impressions on me I started feeling very heavy on my shoulders as I tried to shake it off, I couldn't so I called it out I said anyone here feeling heavy you know you have the spirit of heaviness on you and I described what I was feeling, two young men came out so I laid hands and ministered to them as they were going back to their seats and I saw one of them like in a picture, it appeared before me and disappeared.

In that picture, he was looking for something so I called him back and I said Sir, are you looking for something desperately? he said yes that he is actually looking for a wife so we prayed and guess what? the next day he got connected to someone who is his wife, he explained how he had suffered in the hands of different women but

God gave him his own wife and not a knife.

9.

Confirmations: Confirmation is simply verification or final proof of something. So whatever God tells or shows us to do, He will always give us a word from His Word to stand on or act on. Then, He will confirm it to us- oftentimes through repetition. Confirmation is also the sacrament by which Catholics receive a special outpouring of the Holy Spirit. Through Confirmation, the Holy Spirit gives them the increased ability to practice their Catholic faith in every aspect of their lives and to witness Christ in every situation.

For example, when God was calling me to ministry I had several confirmations in that season of my life everywhere I went any church I went, no matter how I tried to hide there was this prophecy coming up even when I watch TV when I'm online watching programs on Facebook live they will stop and say you have a calling into the prophetic into healing into deliverance so that's how it works.

So when it comes to confirmations God can give you confirmations without you asking or you can ask him for confirmation just to be sure that is the one talking to you. For example, Gideon asked God for confirmation in the Bible but in the case of pharaoh he didn't ask God just gave him a confirmation by repeating the dream twice

Testimony 3

When I met my wife I wanted to confirm if she was truly my wife so I prayed and asked God to show me a confirmation. That same night as I slept I had a dream where she was dressing up in a wedding gown. I saw her hairstyle in detail and the design of her wedding gown so later on in our relationship I told her just about the hairstyle and dress design but didn't tell her the reason. She confirmed the hairstyle and wedding dress in shock. That same week my mother had a dream and saw my wife to be in a dream. When she called me, she described her to a t, she had never met her before or even seen her photograph my mother is a praying woman

10.

Prophets: God speaks to us individually, but He also speaks to His children collectively through His prophets. God used prophets in biblical times to relay His messages and teach His children. Today, God is still calling prophets to fulfill their heavenly duty of relaying His messages to His people. Prophets receive direction from God to help people navigate spiritually along with physical challenges and situations.

Amos 3:7 (KJV)

Surely the Lord GOD will do nothing, but he revealeth his secret unto his servants the prophets.

2Kings 4:8

8 And it fell on a day, that Elisha passed to Shunem, where was a great woman; and she constrained him to eat bread. And so it was, that as oft as he passed by, he turned in thither to eat bread

2Kings 4:16-17

16 And he said, About this season, according to the time of life, thou shalt embrace a son. And she said, Nay, my lord, thou man of God, do not lie unto thine handmaid.

17 And the woman conceived, and bare a son at that season that Elisha had said unto her, according to the time of life.

Testimony 4

God still uses his prophets today. One of the confirmations that I got before going into ministry was through a prophet. I went to the church and he called me out and prophesied over me that God was calling me into the ministry and gave full details; this was actually recorded. God has also used me to prophesy to several other people

Testimony 5

There was a young lady who came to our church one day and I prophesied to her that she will get a job she never applied for and she did not believe or understand it, a few weeks later she came to give a testimony that she was made a manager in a big company which controls a lot of buildings in London.

She was working at a checkout where this lady saw her, liked her and gave her a card to call and the rest was history, no interview no application just like that and God can do the same for you.

> **And did I mention she didn't know anything about this job but it came with training and pay while she was being trained? Glory to God!**

11.

Experiences/Circumstances: God often uses circumstances as teachable moments. But although these experiences may be trying; God uses them for our good, to edify and lead us in the right direction.

A popular example of God communicating through experiences was observed in the life of Moses. From the encounter with the burning bush, to the Egyptian plagues, to the leading of his people through the wilderness to the promised land, the life of Moses was filled with spiritual messages sent from God.

> Pay attention to the experiences and circumstances you find yourself in life especially those that continuously repeat themselves, that could be God trying to draw your attention

12.

People: Put simply, God uses human channels to speak words of prophecy, tongues and interpretation and words of wisdom, knowledge or just to encourage us. He can even use a little child or even a stranger to speak to you

13.

Knowing that you know:

This is when you know that you know but don't know how you know but you just that you know.

Matthew 12:25

And Jesus knew their thoughts, and said unto them, every kingdom divided against itself is brought to desolation; and every city or house divided against itself shall not stand:

14. Gifts: here God uses the nine gifts of the Holy Spirit to speak to us.

The Gifts are divided into three categories:

2. GIFTS TO SAY: Prophecy, Tongues and Interpretation of Tongues.

3. GIFTS TO KNOW: The Word of Wisdom, The Word of Knowledge and The Discerning of Spirits.

4. GIFTS TO DO: The Gift of Faith, The Gifts of Healing and The Working of Miracles.

How To Hear From God Everyday

1 Cor 12:1-12

1 Now concerning spiritual gifts, brethren, I would not have you ignorant.

2 Ye know that ye were Gentiles, carried away unto these dumb idols, even as ye were led.

3 Wherefore I give you to understand, that no man speaking by the Spirit of God calleth Jesus accursed: and that no man can say that Jesus is the Lord, but by the Holy Ghost.

4 Now there are diversities of gifts, but the same Spirit.

5 And there are differences of administrations, but the same Lord.

6 And there are diversities of operations, but it is the same God which worketh all in all.

7 But the manifestation of the Spirit is given to every man to profit withal.

8 For to one is given by the Spirit the word of wisdom; to another the word of knowledge by the same Spirit;

9 To another faith by the same Spirit; to another the gifts of healing by the same Spirit;

10 To another the working of miracles; to another prophecy; to another discerning of spirits; to another divers kinds of tongues; to another the interpretation of tongues:

11 But all these worketh that one and the selfsame Spirit, dividing to every man severally as he will.

12 For as the body is one, and hath many members, and all the members of that one body, being many, are one body: so also is Christ.

15.

Urim and Thummim: In the Hebrew Bible, the Urim and the Thummim (meaning uncertain, possibly "Lights and Perfections"), are elements of the hoshen, the breastplate worn by the High Priest attached to the ephod.

They are connected with divination in general, and cleromancy in particular. Most bible scholars suspect that the phrase refers to a set of two objects used by the high priest to answer a question or reveal the will of God.

The Urim and the Thummim first appear in Exodus 28:30, where they are named for inclusion on the breastplate to be worn by Aaron in the holy place: Exodus 28:30 KJV And thou shalt put in the breastplate of judgment the Urim and the Thummim; and they shall be upon Aaron's heart, when he goeth in before the LORD: and Aaron shall bear the judgment of the children of Israel upon his heart before the LORD continually.

So the Urim and Thummim was an instrument prepared by God to assist man in obtaining revelation from the Lord and in translating languages.

It usually gave a yes or no answer.

1Sam 28:6

And when Saul inquired of the LORD, the LORD answered him not, neither by dreams, nor by Urim, nor by prophets.

Since the Urim is no longer in use, in a spiritual sense, since it is usually put in the breastplate which is close to the heart, so when I want to hear from God using Urim or Thummim, I look out for the feeling of peace in my heart being Urim or feeling of disturbance being Thummim.

16.

Revelations and Rhema: Revelation is when something that was hidden becomes known.

God can give you a revelation about something that you never knew about before. Sometimes when reading the word of God, you suddenly see a different meaning. Sometimes you get a rhema word. In this case, it appears as if a particular verse jumps out from the page at you.

17

Votes - casting of lots: This makes reference to a term called "Unconditional election" (also known as unconditional grace).

In order to know God's mind, the apostles cast lots or voted to find out who would replace Judas.

Acts 1:21-26

21 Wherefore of these men which have companied with us all the time that the Lord Jesus went in and out among us,

22 Beginning from the baptism of John, unto that same day that he was taken up from us, must one be ordained to be a witness with us of his resurrection.

23 And they appointed two, Joseph called Barsabas, who was surnamed Justus, and Matthias.

24 And they prayed, and said, Thou, Lord, which knowest the hearts of all men, shew whether of these two thou hast chosen,

25 That he may take part of this ministry and apostleship, from which Judas by transgression fell, that he might go to his own place.

26 And they gave forth their lots; and the lot fell upon Matthias; and he was numbered with the eleven apostles.

This system is used in some churches when choosing their leaders. The Catholics use it to choose the next Pope.

18

Tests:

1 John 4:11

Beloved, do not believe every spirit, but test the spirits, whether they are of God; because many false prophets have gone out into the world.

When God gave Gideon an assignment, He tested God.

Judges 6:37-40

[36] And Gideon said unto God, If thou wilt save Israel by mine hand, as thou hast said,

How To Hear From God Everyday

^{37} Behold, I will put a fleece of wool on the floor; and if the dew be on the fleece only, and it be dry upon all the earth beside, then shall I know that thou wilt save Israel by mine hand, as thou hast said.

^{38} And it was so: for he rose up early on the morrow, and thrust the fleece together, and wringed the dew out of the fleece, a bowl full of water.

^{39} And Gideon said unto God, Let not thine anger be hot against me, and I will speak but this once: let me prove, I pray thee, but this once with the fleece; let it now be dry only upon the fleece, and upon all the ground let there be dew.

^{40} And God did so that night: for it was dry upon the fleece only, and there was dew on all the ground.

Gideon tested God, you too can test every spirit. you can test God to find out for sure if God is talking to you.

God is not angry when we put him to the test. We should test every spirit including the spirit of God.

> So what is that thing that you want to know for sure? ask God now test the spirit now ask God for a sign now

19.

Signs and wonders:

A sign points us to God while a wonder makes us wow and wonder about God. They can be in the form of healing, miracles, earthquakes, rainbow or volcanoes. It can be anything that God wants to use to point us towards him or to make us wonder. It can also be a miracle.

20.

Interpretations: Interpretation is simply the act of explaining, reframing, or otherwise showing your own understanding of something. One of the most iconic of all dreams in the Bible are those that Joseph had and those he interpreted for Pharaoh. Our dreams can give us hope. And we can see from Joseph's life that sometimes our dreams have both an immediate result and a long-term outcome. However, we need the Divine wisdom of God to help us interpret them, so if it's in His will that we know it.

Genesis 40:8 KJV And they said unto him, We have dreamed a dream, and there is no interpreter of it. And Joseph said unto them, Do not interpretations belong to God? tell me, I pray for you.

> It was when Joseph interpreted their dreams that the hidden messages where revealed.

God can speak through dark sayings or symbols which require interpretation or even through tongues which require interpretation so the message from God will come when the hidden message is revealed.

Testimony 6

In 2015. I believe, I was ministering in India when the baptism of the Holy Spirit fell on the congregation and there was this particular lady who began to speak in tongues.

Even the pastor's daughter who invited me began to speak in tongues for the first time but this lady spoke in tongues for a very long time and I perceive in my spirit that God was bringing a message to the church but there was no one to interpret so I felt led by the Holy Spirit to hold this woman's hand.

As she continued to speak I was interpreting in English and the interpreter was interpreting in Tamil language and after that episode the church glorified God and they said this is what they have been expecting as they were fasting, praying and seeking God.

God decided to speak to them through tongues and interpretation which give them meaning

21.

Symbols:

A symbol is something that represents something else for example the dove is used to represent the Holy Spirit. So God can use symbols to speak to us in a particular season.

God uses Symbols to communicate with us so that we will dig deep in His Word, and get to know Him, and understand the Price that He has paid for us. So that we will see that He has laid out the future for us and that we can have confidence in what He has done in the past that will enable our faith for what He is planning for the future.

22.

Witnesses/Inward witness: In the Bible, a witness is someone who sees something amazing or important. If this person begins to share what they've seen, we call this "bearing witness." Moreover, God doesn't communicate with us the way we communicate with one another. He communicates from His Spirit to your spirit, and then your spirit communicates what you hear to your mind. That is what we call an inward witness. It is very similar to a thought or a prompting. It's very subtle and requires a closeness with God and regular practice to hear it more quickly and clearly.

Romans 8:16 "The Spirit itself beareth witness with our spirit, that we are the children of God."

23.

Messengers/Angels: Angels are God's messengers, so it's important for them to be able to communicate well. Depending on what type of mission God gives them, angels may deliver messages in a variety of different ways, including speaking or writing. So in Scripture, we see that God uses angels to direct, encourage, protect, and instruct His people. Just like He uses dreams to bless us, God uses angels in our lives.

Hebrews 1:14 "Are they not all ministering spirits, sent forth to minister for them who shall be heirs of salvation?"

> Angels appear to us in live or in dreams sometimes, they do not always appear as supernatural beings rather they appear as men of God or ministers of the gospel. sometimes these are the angels attached to those ministries that come to minister to you.

Testimony 7

When God called me into the ministry I had this particular Angel that visited me a lot. This Angel I call him the *healing Angel* always appeared in the form of a renowned man of God known all over the world for healing he would come and visit me, teach me and take me to places all in my dream, sometimes in visions.

The angels sometimes do more than bring you a message, sometimes they impart on you.

Testimony 8

I remember one of my trips to India when I was praying and fasting for God show Himself strong and an Angel visited me, he imparted on me, he put his two hands on my two hands and it was like the feeling of electrocution.

When I jumped up out of that trance the table, plate of food, cup, in fact everything in front of me was scattered because I jumped up because the encounter was very real.

When I got to India I was preaching and I had forgotten about this encounter then suddenly they brought this deaf and dumb woman in front of me and believe me when I tell you my heart sunk.

I was afraid and concerned because during that time I had never prayed for any deaf person or dumb person and they started hearing or speaking.

How To Hear From God Everyday

As I was contemplating on what to do, I remembered that encounter when the Angel visited me and placed two of his hands on my hands and said to me when you get there pray for them like this, so I put two of my hands on her two ears and I said "you spirit of deafness, dumbness, infirmities, sickness and disease I command you to lose her and let her go in the mighty name of Jesus."

I continued to pray this prayer thinking that the woman wasn't healed.

It took the interpreter to stop me to say that she was healed because each time I would pray and stop and ask you if she could hear, she would shake her head left to right.

I thought that meant no, not realizing that culturally that's how Indians move their head in the affirmative.

So it became something to laugh about later, but God did heal her. she began to speak, she began to hear and then they went around looking for any deaf person they could find.

We began to have deaf people service. Glory to God!

Hebrews 13:2

"Be not forgetful to entertain strangers: for thereby some have entertained angels unawares."

> **Sometimes we meet strangers and they turn out to be Angels on divine assignment.**

24.

Men and Women of God: The most important reason we need men and women of God, widely known as pastors, is because Christ has commanded them to be heralds of the Word of God. It is fundamental to the office of pastor to deliver, expound, and explain God's Word to His people. This task is so foundational that it is common to refer to a pastor as "preacher."

> In most cases when we go to church and the pastor is preaching though he's preaching a general message it becomes very particular to us and to everyone else.
>
> We feel as though God has spoken to us for that week for that moment in that season for a particular reason.

25.

Pictures: Based on research, imagery is notably the most expressive way to communicate, which is why it is often said that 'a picture tells a thousand words'.

Perhaps this is why God communicates in this way so often in the Scriptures, particularly in the Old Testament where dreams and visions comprise ⅓ of the content.

Moreover, the most significant reason God speaks symbolically to us through pictures is because pictures are the language of the heart.

Pictures move our emotions and God wants very much to engage our feelings and connect intimately with our hearts.

Jeremiah 23:18 KJV *For who hath stood in the counsel of the LORD, and hath perceived and heard his word? who hath marked his word, and heard it?*

This can happen as snap pictures they can suddenly appear in front of your eyes and disappear or appear in your heart as a picture and that picture tells 1000 stories.

Sometimes God can show you a picture of someone sick, praying, dancing or picture of a body part it's simply means God wants to do something about it that's why he's Showing you for he reveals to redeem and not to destroy

26.

Promptings and feelings: God speaks through impressions in our emotions. This can either look like feeling in our own soul what someone else is experiencing, or feeling what the Lord feels for someone to whom we are ministering.

Sometimes promptings work as if you are being constantly reminded and nudged to do something.

27.

The Holy Spirit: Put simply, the Holy Spirit is God's mouthpiece to believers. The Holy Spirit does not speak on His own. Like Christ, this member of the Trinity has willingly submitted to the authority of the Father. Everything He communicates to us is directly from the Father, for the gospel of John 16:13 says:

John 16:13 KJV Howbeit when he, the Spirit of truth, is come, he will guide you into all truth: for he shall not speak of himself; but whatsoever he shall hear, that shall he speak: and he will shew you things to come.

> As you continue to practice hearing from God over time you would master how the Holy Spirit communicates specifically to you.

Acts 8:29

"Then the Spirit said to Philip, "Go near and overtake this chariot."

Acts 10:19

"As Peter continued to reflect on the vision, the Spirit said to him, "Behold, three men are looking for you."

> **The Holy Spirit is God's mouthpiece to believers**

28.

Messages:

We primarily hear from God by regularly spending time reading the Bible and obeying what it says. The Bible is God's message to humankind. Everything we need to know to live the Christian life is already in the Bible.

How To Hear From God Everyday

As we spend time meditating on his Word, God reveals his truth to us.

2 Timothy 3:16-17 *KJV All scripture is given by inspiration of God, and is profitable for doctrine, for reproof, for correction, for instruction in righteousness: That the man of God may be perfect, thoroughly furnished unto all good works.*

God can also speak to you when you listen to recorded messages or live messages God has a way of taking those words and personalizing them for you another way God speaks is through sent messages it could be through letters and it could even be a text message just as in my case; a text message saved my life read the testimony below.

Testimony 9

In 2004 I was so depressed and suicidal nothing was working for me and I was so low, I decided to take my life so I climbed a tree with a rope and just when I was about to put the rope over my neck a text message came into my phone.

I thought and I strongly believe I had emptied my pocket. I had a strong feeling to reach out and read that message though I was in tears. I never wanted to. I cannot explain how I reached out for my phone. I read the message, and this is what the message said: ***There is a place called tomorrow, the road to it is perseverance and the door through it is determination.*** Then I knew that God was speaking to me I lost every urge to hang myself and I tried calling back that number it never went through I replied to the message, it said message not sent. I'm still alive and I thank God for speaking to me and saving my life through a text message

29.

Journalism/ Journaling: Matthew 24:14 KJV And this gospel of the kingdom shall be preached in all the world for a witness unto all nations; and then shall the end come.

Due to technology, the above Scripture is literally being fulfilled as the Gospel proliferates the globe. However, while Satan manipulates the media to spread his evil message like a virus, our Father in heaven also utilizes the media to disseminate His truth via journalism, satellite TV, radio, internet, websites, social media, books, podcasts, movies and music.

God also uses journaling to speak to us and this is when you write down messages in your journal. Write, store, and date them, overtime when you go back to read them, you would understand clearly how God has been speaking to you. I have several dream books where I wrote dreams that God gives me and when I read them now I understand better than I understood when I actually had those dreams several years ago.

30.

Translations: Even though the Bible was originally and primarily written in Hebrew and Greek, we understand that God can still speak to us through His Word translated into English. We pray to God in English, and He speaks to our hearts in return.

There is another type of translation I wish to discuss or talk about this is when people are transported supernaturally by God from one place to the other or their form is changed gloriously.

How To Hear From God Everyday

2 Cor. 12:1-4

1 It is not expedient for me doubtless to glory. I will come to visions and revelations of the Lord.

2 I knew a man in Christ above fourteen years ago, (whether in the body, I cannot tell; or whether out of the body, I cannot tell: God knoweth;) such an one caught up to the third heaven.

3 And I knew such a man, (whether in the body, or out of the body, I cannot tell: God knoweth;)

4 How that he was caught up into paradise, and heard unspeakable words, which it is not lawful for a man to utter.

Apostle was taken up into the third heaven or paradise and He must have heard from God.

Acts 8:39

Now when they came up out of the water, the Spirit of the Lord caught Philip away, so that the eunuch saw him no more; and he went on his way rejoicing.

Philip was transported physically, spiritually. Sometimes, people are transported spiritually only like in out of body experience.

Sometimes, prophets or people with strong prophetic gifts can say they are in your house or a particular place, they can walk, drive or be driven. They can describe fully what and where they translated to looks like while they are in the congregation ministering. They are in two places at the same time.

Testimony 10

When I realized the call of God upon my life there was a period when I was so hungry to move in the supernatural that I began to fast and pray for 40 days. I had an out body experience at Ashburnham prayer place, Patmos lodge, in Battle, United Kingdom. Two angels took me up to heaven OR the second heaven I should say.

The interesting thing was that I communicated with the angels through thoughts. They knew what I was thinking and acted accordingly.

At one point, I became very afraid and asked them to bring me down and they did. On our way back, I saw the stars, the milky way, the earth was like a globe and we descended right through the roof and went back into my body.

I also remember during that season, as I prayed and fasted a voice spoke to me and said you shall receive what you have attained. I had a knock on the door two men {angels} came and handed me over a Bible then I understood that in as much as I wanted to have supernatural grace I also needed a balance of the word of God.

31.

Testimonies

Giving your personal testimony is a way to share the gospel with others by explaining your personal salvation experience. It also gives others an example of how God changes lives.

When a testimony is shared it establishes the fact that God is doing something, saying something and wants to do something over and over. where a testimony or testimonies are continuously shared, more testimonies keep happening because it gives people faith to believe God for more.

testimonies are God speaking and when he speaks it comes to pass

> **Sometimes you hear ministers prophesying, they could say right now I am in your house and at a particular place, that is translation, the person is here and someone else simultaneously.**

32.

Thoughts: God can speak to you through your thoughts, but it comes through your spirit. This is a primary way that God speaks. The ability to tell which thoughts are from God and which thoughts are just from yourself will get easier with experience. So you can talk to God out loud or inside your mind, whichever feels most effective to you. It may be best to find a quiet or private space you can occupy in order to concentrate while you're talking.

Sometimes this can happen as a sharp thought. It is often called God thinks to us some other time you find yourself having a conversation in your thoughts with God he speaks to you in your thoughts and you speak back to him in your thoughts like telepathic thought transmission

33.

Patterns and Repetition: As we read the Bible, we come across patterns. Patterns become recognizable when a reader sees a spiritual truth that is stated in one part of the Bible being repeated in a similar fashion in yet another portion of the Bible. The very fact that God has said something twice means that He wants us to take careful note of what He has said. This is important when we consider what Joseph said to Pharaoh as he interpreted his dreams:

Genesis 41:32 KJV *And for that the dream was doubled unto Pharaoh twice; it is because the thing is established by God, and God will shortly bring it to pass.*

When God gives us the same truth in TWO FORMS we have to take careful note of it. So patterns, by virtue of the same truth being found repeated in two forms at least in two portions in the Bible, demands our careful attention.

So begin to pay attention to the patterns and repetitions in your own life. it could be God speaking to you telling you to do something about this for example in a family where there is a pattern of failure, near success syndrome or anything that keeps repeating itself God is saying something about this

34.

Inspiration: Some biblical texts, such as parts of the Old Testament prophets, seem to have been dictated with the direct voice of God, but other parts are clearly in the writer's own voice, but this does not make one text more "inspired" than the other. Similarly, inspiration may be consciously known by the author, or it may be unconscious. So hence, God is speaking through an instrument, but that instrument is not a mere pen but rather a whole human life and personality as gathered into a particular moment of communication.

Another way this can happen is that something occurs or happens to your life or around you and then you become inspired to do something about it. It is almost as if the incident or occurrence spoke to you to come up with this solution.

Sometimes this could be through that people turn around and have inspiration to do something better so that it never happens to someone else again

Someone was inspired to come up with the microphone, television, telephone, aeroplane to mention but a few.

> **Godly inspiration comes from God**

What have you been inspired to do lately?

35.

Exercising Your senses

For you to keep hearing from God, you need to keep exercising your senses

Hebrews 5:14 KJV

[14] But strong meat belongeth to them that are of full age, even those who by reason of use have their senses exercised to discern both good and evil.

How To Hear From God Everyday

Biology teaches us that we have five natural sciences, these are: sight, smell, sound, taste and touch. God is spirit and they that worship him must worship him in spirit and in truth, in other words we have to communicate with God in spirit to be able to worship him in spirit, so the same way we have 5 senses in the natural we also have 5 senses or more in the soulish realm and five or more senses in this spiritual realm so to say.

> **That is a total of fifteen senses, which means fifteen ways God can communicate to us already.**

The same way we can see, smell, hear sound, taste and touch with our physical senses we can also do the same with these five senses in the realm of our soul for example when you remember what's your favourite food tastes like you could almost taste it there and then but you're not tasting it physically this is you testing it in the realm of the soul when you remember what's your favourite perfume smells like you could almost smell it there and there but the perfume is not there.

Everything that happens in the physical realm can happen in the soulish and spirit realms.

Ezekiel was given a scroll to eat in the spirit it was like honey in his mouth so for us to constantly hear from God in a prophetic way, we need to continuously exercise these senses. overtime it will become easier and clearer.

Ezekiel 3:1-3

1. Moreover he said unto me, Son of man, eat that thou findest; eat this roll, and go speak unto the house of Israel. **2**. So I opened my mouth, and he caused me to eat that roll.

3. And he said unto me, Son of man, cause thy belly to eat, and fill thy bowels with this roll that I give thee.

Then did I eat it; and it was in my mouth as honey for sweetness.

Testimony 11

In one of my encounters with God he opened my spiritual ears and I could hear the angels sing oh what a glorious loud Symphony of the best orchestra.

Sometimes God can activate people's sense of smell, spiritually speaking; when they are worshipping, that is one of the ways of God to communicate to them that His presence is there. Sometimes, it can be a scent of His sweet perfume or fragrance that is nothing from this world.

TEN Hindrances to hearing God's voice and how to overcome them

The section of this book will address ten reasons why people don't hear from God effectively and how to overcome them. I have spent more time dealing with unforgiveness because it is the most common reason I come across as I minister globally

1. **Time and space**

Not creating time and space to hear from God can be a hindrance, you want to hear from God? create time for Him.

2. **Sin**

Sin stands the way of our hearing from God.

"If I have cherished sin in my heart, the Lord would not have listened" [Psalm 66:18] "But your iniquities have separated you from your God; your sins have hidden his face from you so that he will not hear." [Isaiah 59:2].

Quickly check your heart and ask God if there is any sin you need to confess or thing you need to stop doing.

3. Delayed obedience

Whatever God asked you to do that you have not done, could prevent him from speaking further to you until you obey the first instruction.

4. Wrong Expectations

Sometimes we expect God to speak to us in a specific or particular whereas He could already be speaking to us in a way we don't expect. Learn to be open.

One day, a preacher was praying to God to give him a message, he prayed and fasted yet He heard nothing from God. He wanted to know if He should go ahead with a particular project or not. Disappointed that God didn't speak to him, as he ended his fasting and going back to the office, a NIKE SHOE VAN pulled in front of him with a slogan ''just do it''. He obeyed and the result was outstanding

5. God's Timing

Is this the right time for you to hear about that particular thing?

Jesus waited to go to Lazarus until after he died, John 10, much to the dismay of his disciples. But God wanted to do something bigger than heal a sick man – he wanted to raise him from the dead! Jesus was obedient to his Fathers timing.

Is there something else that God wants to speak to you about today? Have I submitted to His agenda plans for only willing to work off my schedule?

6. Relationship

A strong relationship is built on the foundation of communication.

If you want to hear from God easily, start building a strong relationship with him. Just talk to him every opportunity you get and wait for Him to speak back to you

7. Motives /Reason

You must have a pure motive to hear God.

Matthew 5:8

Blessed are the pure in heart: for they shall see God.

When you see God, He will talk to you.

8. Wrong Beliefs

Do you believe that God doesn't speak to us actively anymore that everything we need is in the bible or do you that in addition to the Bible, God still speaks actively.

> **You see what you say and become what you believe.**

Matthew 4:4

4 But he answered and said, It is written, Man shall not live by bread alone, but by every word that proceedeth out of the mouth of God

Proceedeth means words are still proceeding out of God's mouth

9. Limiting God

Don't put God in a box

When we submit our plans and ideas to God and allow the Holy Spirit to bring

His creative solutions to the front, then we're no-longer limiting God to our understanding or ideas. He sees the bigger picture and how it will work out in years to come.

10. Unforgiveness

"And when you stand praying, if you hold anything against anyone, forgive him, so that your Father in heaven may forgive you your sins." [Mark 11:25]

Or "..if you are offering your gift at the altar and there remember that your brother or sister has something against you, leave your gift there … First, go and be reconciled to them; then come and offer your gift." [Matthew 5:23+24]

Taking a few minutes at the start to ask God if there is anything you need to put right with Him or others is good preparation — to deal with stuff clouding your heart & spirit from being fully right with God. If something comes to mind, ask God for forgiveness, or if it's someone else – contact them immediately (if it's convenient for them) or make a note to do as soon as possible.

Note – you are hearing from God, just not on the 'thing' you'd like to hear about from Him.

It may also mean that you need to forgive yourself. At times its easier to forgive someone else but we're harsher on ourselves.

Forgiveness doesn't mean that what 'HE/SHE' did to you was ok. It probably wasn't. Starting down a path of forgiveness (which is sometimes a process) means that you don't want to be bound to them and thus chained yourself, thus stopping God coming to bring His healing and forgiveness.

Some people have been abused, their hearts broken, lied against, cheated on, betrayed, raped or even stolen from. Some have been prevented from having access to their children etc.

When we forgive others, it doesn't mean that God has forgiven them. It doesn't mean they deserve it or asked us for forgiveness. RATHER IT GIVES GOD MORE ROOM TO FIGHT FOR US

Forgiveness is a gift we give ourselves so we are free from the burden unforgiveness brings.

Unforgiveness can lead to anger, bitterness, malice and murder in extreme cases.

It says FOR-GIVE NOT FOR-KEEP

WE ARE MEANT TO GIVE IT NOT KEEP IT.

Also forgive yourself, no matter what you have done, let God down and you repented and confessed it. God has forgiven you, now forgive yourself.

Proverbs 28:13

He that covereth his sins shall not prosper: but whoso confesseth and forsaketh *them* shall have mercy.

Micah 7:19

He will turn again, he will have compassion upon us; he will subdue our iniquities; and thou wilt cast all their sins into the depths of the sea.

PRAYER

My Father my maker, any man or woman living or dead who has offended me hurt me or paid me back evil for the good I rendered onto them I let go and I let you God to handle it. I choose to forgive forget and forge on in Jesus name, Amen.

Sometimes you may have to forgive people over and over until you actually forgive them

Unforgiveness not only stops us from hearing from God it can also prevent us from receiving other things from him like our blessings or even healing.

Testimony 12

Few years ago I was ministering to this lady, she had arthritis in her knees but she wasn't getting healed. As I continued to pray the spirit said to me she has unforgiveness so I asked her if anybody offended her that she hasn't forgiven. she said yes; her dead husband.

I asked how long has your husband been dead? more than 10 years but she still carried unforgiveness which stopped her healing, well we later prayed the forgiveness prayer, she forgave the husband and she got healed instantly.

TESTIMONY 13

When I left my medical career to answer God's call, it didn't go so well with my father. We didn't speak to each other for a long time. I came from a catholic background. One day, I got a phone call that my nephew (my sister's son) was ill. I offered to pray for him but they said he was sleeping so I asked them not to wake him up. I understand he always fell ill and was born with just one testicle. I asked my sister to get some olive oil and apply it on him but they had none. I forgot they were still Catholics.

How To Hear From God Everyday

When I asked what oil they had at home, they said palm oil. I prayed over the phone from London while they were in Nigeria. I asked my sister to apply some red oil on the son after I had prayed and blessed it over the phone.

The next day, he woke up with two of his testicles complete and since then he stopped falling ill frequently. Then something else happened.

When my mother saw what happened, she called me to pray for her. She had arthritis. I was so happy that my own mother would ask me to pray for her. As I opened my mouth to pray over the phone, the spirit said to me, don't pray. I asked why because, this is my own mother. The spirit told me that my mother had unforgiveness towards her brothers which has developed into bitterness, so my prayer would not work unless she forgave.

You see, my mother gave up her education to train her brothers hoping that they will help her train her own kids but she felt abandoned by them later on. So, I told her what the spirit was saying and she confirmed it. I led her through the forgiveness prayer and she was healed instantly.

Here is what the Bible says about bitterness. You can see there is a connection between bitterness and our health

Proverbs 17:22

A merry heart doeth good *like* a medicine: but a broken spirit drieth the bones.

(Dry bones= Arthritis) Emphasis added

FINAL NOTE ON HINDRANCES TO HEARING FROM GOD AND HOW TO OVERCOME THEM.

What We Watch and Listen To

The things we watch or listen to can cloud our minds and cause interferences when it comes to hearing from God.

Have you ever had an experience where you are trying to pray but your mind keeps going to a movie you watched or something you listened to?

This happens a lot with pornography or worldly music. Also avoid strife, fights and quarrels.

This is what the Bible says about the above

2 Timothy 2:19-26

19 Nevertheless the foundation of God standeth sure, having this seal, The Lord knoweth them that are his. And, Let everyone that nameth the name of Christ depart from iniquity.

20 But in a great house there are not only vessels of gold and of silver, but also of wood and of earth; and some to honour, and some to dishonour.

21 If a man therefore purge himself from these, he shall be a vessel unto honour, sanctified, and meet for the master's use, *and* prepared unto every good work.

22 Flee also youthful lusts: but follow righteousness, faith, charity, peace, with them that call on the Lord out of a pure heart.

23 But foolish and unlearned questions avoid, knowing that they do gender strifes.

24 And the servant of the Lord must not strive; but be gentle unto all *men*, apt to teach, patient,

25 In meekness instructing those that oppose themselves; if God peradventure will give them repentance to the acknowledging of the truth;

26 And *that* they may recover themselves out of the snare of the devil, who are taken captive by him at his will.

CHAPTER THREE

How to know God's permissive and perfect will

Introduction

We shall discuss in this chapter, God's divine will, which is his perfect and permissive plan for our lives. We shall shed light on how we can identify God's will for our lives.

What is the will of God?

The Greek word for "will" is thelma, which means "what one wishes or has determined will happen." That is, we are to want God to have His wish, His will and His plans fulfilled. That is, your life and plans should correlate with His.

So put simply, the will of God includes everything that God desires or wishes to happen in heaven and on earth. As a result, He has planned what He wishes to occur. For example, in the first part of the Lord's Prayer, found in the Sermon on the Mount, Jesus teaches us to pray that the Father's will be done on earth as it is in heaven.

Matthew 6:9-10 KJV *After this manner therefore pray ye: Our Father which art in heaven, Hallowed be thy name.*

(10) Thy kingdom come. Thy will be done in earth, as it is in heaven.

However, when some people think about the will of God, they fear that God has already decided every little detail of their life. But that is not the case.

God has not already decided everything in your life. But God does control many aspects of our lives.

He gives us a lot of freedom, but He has also constrained us as written in the book of Acts 16:6-10, which reads:

Acts 16:6-10 KJV Now when they had gone throughout Phrygia and the region of Galatia, and were forbidden of the Holy Ghost to preach the word in Asia,

(7) After they were come to Mysia, they assayed to go into Bithynia: but the Spirit suffered them not.

(8) And they passing by Mysia came down to Troas.

(9) And a vision appeared to Paul in the night; There stood a man of Macedonia, and prayed him, saying, Come over into Macedonia, and help us.

(10) And after he had seen the vision, immediately we endeavoured to go into Macedonia, assuredly gathering

that the Lord had called us to preach the gospel unto them.

So God's will be just like a road. He doesn't care if you walk on the right side, the left side or down the middle. He doesn't care if you jump, skip, jog, walk fast, or even crawl down the road. He doesn't care if you sing or if you are silent as you walk down the road. But He does care if you go astray or leave the road.

He wants you to always stay on the road. Each of us has a different road to travel. The road is God's will for your life. The road will turn and twist and be full of obstacles, but His plan will be accomplished, for your own good and to His glory, but only as long as you don't go astray through the sin and corruption of this world.

It is permissive and perfect

The perfect will of God is God's divine plan for your life: like the kind of spouse to marry, what career or ministry to pursue, and so on. It needs you to be very patient and trust God because He wants to give His best, which has His full blessings, not the second best.

However, God's permissible will does not have His full blessings. In the book of 1 Samuel verse 8, God wanted to be the king of the Israelites but the people saw how other nations had a king and desired one for themselves. They cried and complained to Samuel who went to God in prayer. God permitted them to have a king but then problems started; they experienced one war after the other.

How To Hear From God Everyday

1 Samuel 8:1-22 KJV And it came to pass, when Samuel was old, that he made his sons judges over Israel.

(2) Now the name of his firstborn was Joel; and the name of his second, Abiah: they were judges in Beersheba.

(3) And his sons walked not in his ways, but turned aside after lucre, and took bribes, and perverted judgment.

(4) Then all the elders of Israel gathered themselves together, and came to Samuel unto Ramah,

(5) And said unto him, Behold, thou art old, and thy sons walk not in thy ways: now make us a king to judge us like all the nations.

(6) But the thing displeased Samuel, when they said, Give us a king to judge us. And Samuel prayed unto the LORD.

(7) And the LORD said unto Samuel, Hearken unto the voice of the people in all that they say unto thee: for they have not rejected thee, but they have rejected me, that I should not reign over them.

(8) According to all the works which they have done since the day that I brought them up out of Egypt even unto this day, wherewith they have forsaken me, and served other gods, so do they also unto thee.

(9) Now therefore hearken unto their voice: howbeit yet protest solemnly unto them, and shew them the manner of the king that shall reign over them.

(10) And Samuel told all the words of the LORD unto the people that asked of him a king.

(11) And he said, This will be the manner of the king that shall reign over you: He will take your sons, and appoint them for himself, for his

chariots, and to be his horsemen; and some shall run before his chariots.

(12) And he will appoint him captains over thousands, and captains over fifties; and will set them to ear his ground, and to reap his harvest, and to make his instruments of war, and instruments of his chariots.

(13) And he will take your daughters to be confectionaries, and to be cooks, and to be bakers.

(14) And he will take your fields, and your vineyards, and your oliveyards, even the best of them, and give them to his servants.

(15) And he will take the tenth of your seed, and of your vineyards, and give to his officers, and to his servants.

(16) And he will take your menservants, and your maidservants, and your goodliest young men, and your asses, and put them to his work.

(17) He will take the tenth of your sheep: and ye shall be his servants.

(18) And ye shall cry out in that day because of your king which ye shall have chosen you; and the LORD will not hear you in that day.

(19) Nevertheless the people refused to obey the voice of Samuel; and they said, Nay; but we will have a king over us;

(20) That we also may be like all the nations; and that our king may judge us, and go out before us, and fight our battles.

(21) And Samuel heard all the words of the people, and he rehearsed them in the ears of the LORD.

(22) And the LORD said to Samuel, Hearken unto their voice, and make them a king. And Samuel said unto the men of Israel, Go ye every man unto his city.

So God's permissible will always have consequences because God would only have given you what you wanted because you were crying or praying day and night over the issue, due to the fact that you were not patient enough to wait for His timing. So in essence, His permissible will teaches us to be patient and faithful because He always knows what's best for us.

His will for us

We as Christians have a distinct advantage over unbelievers when it comes to facing decisions. We not only know that our sovereign God has already planned the way that is best for us, but we have infallible information about his priorities that will help us follow his plan. We have the inspired Word of God. And God specifically mentions at least five things in his Word that are part of his will for our lives. He actually says, for all practical purposes, "This is my will for you."

These five things have direct bearing on many of life's decisions. Let's look at them:

Salvation: The first point in God's plan for your life, therefore, is that you be saved. You must start here if you ever hope to know the rest of God's will. Admit your sin. Agree that there is nothing you have ever done or can do that will commend you to an infinitely righteous God. Believe that Jesus Christ died in your place and for your sins. Then put your trust in him as your personal sin bearer and Saviour. God will forgive your sins, assure you that heaven is your destiny, and set you on an exciting new road of peace and purpose here and now.

Holiness: It is God's will that we be holy. The word sanctification means holiness, consecration and dedication to God. The Word of God makes it clear that to have sexual relations outside the bond of marriage is impure, and Christians are to abstain from such practices. A fellow never needs to question whether or not God wants him to have sexual relations with his girlfriend. God has already made his will know in that matter. He always desires purity.

Attitude of gratitude: This is one statement of God's will that many Christians find difficult to accept. They know they should thank God for the good things that happen to them, but they cannot bring themselves to thank him for the problems. They are convinced that some circumstances give them a perfect right to grumble, gripe, and complain. The first thing God wants each of them to do is to thank him genuinely and sincerely for the problem, and to thank him for another opportunity to grow spiritually and to learn more about his all-sufficient grace. That thankful spirit may be the very thing God will use to relieve the tension and make the situation more tolerable.

Do you want to know God's will for your life? It is that you always give thanks, in every situation, whether good or bad, for everything.

Submission: It is God's will for us to submit ourselves to the laws of the land. This is one way he can shut the mouths of those who oppose the gospel. This God-willed submissiveness to authority reaches beyond our attitude toward government, however. Employees are exhorted to be submissive to their employers. Wives are encouraged to be submissive to their husbands. Believers generally are asked to submit to the spiritual leaders of their local churches. as a matter of fact, all of us develop a submissive spirit toward each other.

If you are wondering whether God wants you to stand up for your rights, or argue for your opinion, or insist on doing things your way, then you have your answer. God wants you to be submissive.

Suffering: Twice, Peter mentions suffering according to the will of God.

1 Peter 3:17 KJV For it is better, if the will of God be so, that ye suffer for well doing, than for evil doing.

1 Peter 4:19 KJV Wherefore let them that suffer according to the will of God commit the keeping of their souls to him in well doing, as unto a faithful Creator.

Now these verses should not be misunderstood. They do not say precisely that it is God's will for every Christian to suffer, but they certainly imply that it could be. And if we do suffer, it ought to be for doing good rather than for sinful attitudes and actions.

The truth of the matter is that If we are living godly lives in this godless world, we are bound to experience some forms of opposition to it. That is God's will, for he knows that it can draw us closer to him, make us appreciate him more, depend on him to a greater extent, and strengthen our spiritual lives.

If we are breezing through life without any opposition from the people of the world, one of two things is probably true—either we are not living godly lives, or else they cannot see it. Because If they do see it, some of them are definitely going to strike out against us and cause us problems. God says so.

So in conclusion to this chapter, these are the declarations of God's will for our lives. God wants us to be saved, pure, thankful, submissive, and ready to suffer. So I implore you to seek God's wisdom in applying them to the next decision you face. Be blessed as you do so in Jesus name. We shall move on to hearing of God's voice along with his choices over our lives.

CHAPTER FOUR

Hearing God's voice/choice

Introduction

This chapter will shed light on the audible perception of God's voice and what it signifies in our lives. It shall also discuss His choice over our lives.

What it signifies to hear his voice

John 10:27 KJV My sheep hear my voice, and I know them, and they follow me:

Every single true believer knows the voice of God, it's just whether or not they actually attribute it to God. God has promised to guide us if we listen. He tells us not to listen to our own understanding but to acknowledge Him in all our ways. So If you do what he says, He will make your paths straight, for the book of Proverbs 3:6 says:

Proverbs 3:6 KJV In all thy ways acknowledge him, and he shall direct thy paths.

God wants to guide you because he knows what is best for us in every situation. So in essence, things go right when we listen. When David inquired of the Lord, listened to His response and executed the detailed battle plans God gave him, he won great victories over his enemies:

2 Samuel 5:17-25 KJV But when the Philistines heard that they had anointed David king over Israel, all the Philistines came up to seek David; and David heard of it, and went down to the hold.

(18) The Philistines also came and spread themselves in the valley of Rephaim.

(19) And David enquired of the LORD, saying, Shall I go up to the Philistines? wilt thou deliver them into mine hand? And the LORD said unto David, Go up: for I will doubtless deliver the Philistines into thine hand.

(20) And David came to Baalperazim, and David smote them there, and said, The LORD hath broken forth upon mine enemies before me, as the breach of waters. Therefore he called the name of that place Baalperazim.

(21) And there they left their images, and David and his men burned them.

(22) And the Philistines came up yet again, and spread themselves in the valley of Rephaim.

(23) And when David enquired of the LORD, he said, Thou shalt not go up; but fetch a compass behind them, and come upon them over against the mulberry trees.

(24) And let it be, when thou hearest the sound of a going in the tops of the mulberrytrees, that then thou shalt bestir thyself: for then shall the LORD go out before thee, to smite the host of the Philistines.

(25) And David did so, as the LORD had commanded him; and smote the Philistines from Geba until thou come to Gazer.

However, that things go right when we listen, does not mean they are always easy. When Jesus submitted to the will of the Father in Gethsemane it surely wasn't easy. It took Him to the cross. But it was right; and it lead to the defeat of Satan and the salvation of the world. Listening leads us to Christ himself. Jesus said in John 6:45:

John 6:45 KJV It is written in the prophets, And they shall be all taught of God. Every man therefore that hath heard, and hath learned of the Father, cometh unto me.

When the Father speaks He directs us to His Son because all the answers to life's questions are found in Him. The greatest benefit of listening to God is that we are directed by the Father to the Son and to the life He gives. Without His leading life is impossible. With His leading, life is full of purpose, provision, and His presence.

His choice over our lives

Matthew 22:14 KJV For many are called, but few are chosen.

When it comes to the preaching of the gospel many are called by the word preached, but that some believe is a matter of God's choice. Salvation depends on God's choice and not man's. That choice includes Jesus' calling His disciples. This was not, however, a mere choosing of men for office. Such an explanation is too superficial. We read, in John 6:70 that:

John 6:70 KJV Jesus answered them, Have not I chosen you twelve, and one of you is a devil?

Furthermore, Jesus says, in John 15:16 that:

John 15:16 KJV Ye have not chosen me, but I have chosen you, and ordained you, that ye should go and bring forth fruit, and that your fruit should remain: that whatsoever ye shall ask of the Father in my name, he may give it you.

So Jesus' words are clear. It is He who chose His own. The disciples did not make their decision for Christ. Christ, according to the will of God, chose them. The fruit they should bear as His servants, through faith and by the labour of the gospel, was also His and not theirs. He ordained them, not only to office, but to be fruitful.

The fruit of their labour in the gathering of the church was also ordained of God in Christ. So Jesus teaches God's choice in Him unto salvation and faith. It is a false Christ of man's invention who offers himself to all for man's sovereign choice to accept or reject him. Faith is not a decision but a gift of God. Be blessed as you move on to the next and final chapter titled Impartation in the mighty name of Jesus. Amen.

CHAPTER FIVE

Impartation

Introduction

In this chapter, we shall shed light on the meaning of the meaning of impartation along with its spiritual importance. Be blessed as you conclude this book in the mighty name of Jesus. Amen.

What is impartation?

The word "impart "or "impartation "is from the Greek "Metadidomi "and it means to "hand over or give over", this implies the sharing or transfer of an item or spiritual abilities from one person to the other. Impartation, then, is the act of giving or granting something. Impartation, then, is the act of giving something or granting something. Both material and immaterial things can be imparted. The Bible talks about things being imparted to believers:

· **Material goods**: 1 Timothy 6:18 KJV That they do good, that they be rich in good works, ready to distribute, willing to communicate;

· **Spiritual gifts**: Romans 1:11 KJV For I long to see you, that I may impart unto you some spiritual gift, to the end ye may be established;

· **Wisdom**: Proverbs 29:15 KJV The rod and reproof give wisdom: but a child left to himself bringeth his mother to shame.

· **The message of the gospel**: 1 Thessalonians 2:8 KJV So being affectionately desirous of you, we were willing to have imparted unto you, not the gospel of God only, but also our own souls, because ye were dear unto us.

So some groups of people use the term impartation theologically to refer to a transfer of righteousness to believers in the process of sanctification.

Divine impartation

Divine impartation is a means of spiritual transfer of the spiritual gifts brought about by the power of the Holy Spirit. This is the ability to give unto others that which God has given to us either sovereignly, or through other anointed vessels of God. A divine impartation may come upon us directly from God to enable us to do what we've not been able to do before.

Moreover, when we are born again, the Holy Spirit comes to indwell us. We are further empowered when we receive the baptism of the Holy Spirit. And we as believers, should continue to receive impartations of the Spirit's power throughout our faith.

So divine impartation may also be defined as a reception of supernatural power from God, which brings a definite positive difference in a person's life or ministry. Impartation often refers to receiving a spiritual gift or a specific anointing. An example would be having a healing evangelist lay hands on you and noticing a definite increase in the healing power flowing from the evangelist into you.

In addition to this, Christ said that the Holy Spirit would flow through the one who thirsts for it. So we should actively and relentlessly pursue being continually filled with the power of God's Spirit. There are currently two major ways of receiving this divine anointing or impartation, and they are:

Laying on of Hands: This is relatively self-explanatory, however, few may question whether impartation through the laying on of hands has any scriptural reference.

Indeed, there are, in both the Old and New Testament. In the Old Testament Joshua received an impartation from Moses in Deuteronomy 34:9 which reads:

Deuteronomy 34:9 KJV And Joshua the son of Nun was full of the spirit of wisdom; for Moses had laid his hands upon him: and the children of Israel hearkened unto him, and did as the LORD commanded Moses.

And in the New Testament, Paul told Timothy to stir up the gift of God which is in you through the laying on of my hands:

2 Timothy 1:6 KJV Wherefore I put thee in remembrance that thou stir up the gift of God, which is in thee by the putting on of my hands.

Praying/Waiting on God: The Church received the baptism of the Holy Spirit on the day of Pentecost. However, this kind of praying and waiting on God should not just be a one-off experience. We see the church praying and receiving an infilling of the Holy Spirit again in Acts 4:24-31, which reads:

Acts 4:24-31 KJV And when they heard that, they lifted up their voice to God with one accord, and said, Lord, thou art God, which hast made heaven, and earth, and the sea, and all that in them is:

(25) Who by the mouth of thy servant David hast said, Why did the heathen

rage, and the people imagine vain things?

(26) The kings of the earth stood up, and the rulers were gathered together against the Lord, and against his Christ.

(27) For of a truth against thy holy child Jesus, whom thou hast anointed, both Herod, and Pontius Pilate, with the Gentiles, and the people of Israel, were gathered together,

(28) For to do whatsoever thy hand and thy counsel determined before to be done.

(29) And now, Lord, behold their threatening: and grant unto thy servants, that with all boldness they may speak thy word,

(30) By stretching forth thine hand to heal; and that signs and wonders may be done by the name of thy holy child Jesus.

(31) And when they had prayed, the place was shaken where they were assembled together; and they were all filled with the Holy Ghost, and they spake the word of God with boldness.

Its spiritual importance

The practice of impartation is based on the idea that specially chosen and anointed believers have the special ability to share, give or impart the spiritual gifts they have, with others.

The impartation of God is for a purpose and is not only for pastors. It is for every child of God. Samuel anointed David in the midst of his brethren and from that day forward the spirit of God came mightily upon him. Where you have failed before, you will no longer fail. Even God imparted his divine grace upon Jesus before he began ministry. Below are the two major importance or benefits of spiritual impartation:

How To Hear From God Everyday

Understanding: The most important thing a believer requires after salvation is an understanding of what has been done for him in Christ. If he lacks this understanding there will be a limitation in what he can achieve. So where it concerns impartation of understanding, the focus is in the faculty of the mind. For it is by the mind men receive knowledge.

Ephesians 1:17-20 KJV That the God of our Lord Jesus Christ, the Father of glory, may give unto you the spirit of wisdom and revelation in the knowledge of him:

(18) The eyes of your understanding being enlightened; that ye may know what is the hope of his calling, and what the riches of the glory of his inheritance in the saints,

(19) And what is the exceeding greatness of his power to us-ward who believe, according to the working of his mighty power,

(20) Which he wrought in Christ, when he raised him from the dead, and set him at his own right hand in the heavenly places…

Spiritual Gift: This is the most popular and most sought after blessing. It usually occurs by one man laying hands on another for transfer of spiritual ability. Also used to transfer spiritual gifts, is words. One major thing to see where impartation is concerned is that this transfer doesn't happen without a relationship.

There is no single place where a man was imparted with spirituals where he didn't have a current, ongoing relationship with the person who imparted him. We have no single example.

How To Hear From God Everyday

Genesis 27:24-30 KJV And he said, Art thou my very son Esau? And he said, I am.

(25) And he said, Bring it near to me, and I will eat of my son's venison, that my soul may bless thee. And he brought it near to him, and he did eat: and he brought him wine, and he drank.

(26) And his father Isaac said unto him, Come near now, and kiss me, my son.

(27) And he came near, and kissed him: and he smelled the smell of his raiment, and blessed him, and said, See, the smell of my son is as the smell of a field which the LORD hath blessed:

(28) Therefore God give thee of the dew of heaven, and the fatness of the earth, and plenty of corn and wine:

(29)Let people serve thee, and nations bow down to thee: be lord over thy brethren, and let thy mother's sons bow down to thee: cursed be everyone that curseth thee, and blessed be he that blesseth thee.

(30) And it came to pass, as soon as Isaac had made an end of blessing Jacob, and Jacob was yet scarce gone out from the presence of Isaac his father, that Esau his brother came in from his hunting.

Thy will be done

So in conclusion to this final chapter and enlightening book, the Lord's simple requests often serve as stepping stones to life's most wonderful blessings. Often, God's greatest blessings come as a result of our willingness to do something that appears very insignificant, so this is why it's fundamentally vital to always seek and listen to His voice.

How To Hear From God Everyday

For it is God's will that we live righteous and upright lives to reap the rewards of Peace, Joy and Prosperity. I pray that you hear from the Lord today and be blessed abundantly in the mighty name of Jesus. Amen.

Reference list

Charity K. 3 Reasons God Speaks in Symbols, September 27, 2017,

https://www.cwgministries.org/blogs/3-reasons-god-speaks-symbols

Cherly S. 8 Ways God speaks to Us Today, 2021,

https://www.thechristianalarm.com/8-ways-god-speaks-to-us-today/

"Hearing the Voice of God." The Meeting Place Ministries, 2021,

http://www.tmpmin.org/Inspirational-Messages/ArticleID/61/Hearing-the-voice-of-God

"How does God speak?" Institute in Basic Life Principles, 2020,

https://iblp.org/questions/how-does-god-speak

"Is God Speaking to You in Your Dreams?" Bibles for Israel and the Messianic Bible Project, 2021,

https://free.messianicbible.com/feature/god_speaks_in_dreams/

Richard S. This is the Will of God, April 19th 2005,

https://bible.org/seriespage/9-will-god

"What is the baptism of the Holy Spirit?" Gotquestions.org, April 26, 2021,

https://www.gotquestions.org/Spirit-baptism.html

Altar call to receive Christ

The greatest blessing, we can receive from our Lord in heaven is the blessing of salvation.

To receive this, you must surrender your life to Jesus and accept Him as your Lord and personal saviour.

If you would like to do so now, kindly say this prayer with your whole heart.

"Dear Lord Jesus Christ, thank you for dying for the remission of my sins on the cross of Calvary.

I believe you are the son of God, that you died for my sins, were buried and rose on the third day and the you are seated at the right hand of Our father in heaven.

I believe you will come back again to take the saints to heaven.

How To Hear From God Everyday

With my heart I believe these things and that you are my Lord and personal Saviour.

Please forgive me my sins and I also forgive others right now because you first forgave me and if I don't forgive, you won't forgive me either. Write my name in the book of life.

Come into my life and become my Lord and personal saviour.

With my mouth I confess that you are my Lord and saviour of my soul

Fill me with your Holy Spirit and grant me the grace to lead a life righteousness, holiness and of fire.

In Jesus Christ name I pray, Amen."

If you prayed this prayer and really meant it, I Believe you have received the miracle of salvation, prayerfully seek a Bible believing, Holy Spirit filled Church and become a member there.

Prayer Points

1. Lord Jesus, I come before you today because I want to hear your voice. I want you to always speak to me, just like you speak to the Prophets of the old, the same way you people your sons and daughters of Zion who have shunned the world to follow you, I pray that you will speak to me clearly in the name of Jesus.

2. I unlock every of my spiritual sense organs right now in the name of Jesus. My spiritual eyes are opened, my spiritual ears are opened in the name of Jesus. I pray that your spirit will come upon me, the spirit that will quicken my mortal body, your spirit that you have promised us in the book of Acts of Apostles, I pray that you will descend it upon me right now in the name of Jesus.

How To Hear From God Everyday

3. Lord Jesus, I pray that when you speak to be it will be clear, the grace for me to identify your voice, I pray that you give it to me in the name of Jesus. The grace to know when you speak, the power to understand what you say, I pray that you will give it to me in the name of Jesus.

4. Father Lord, I come against every power of sin in my life. Every sin that will stop my spiritual connectivity to you. Every sin that will stop me from hearing your voice Clearly, I pray that you will take it away in the name of Jesus. Father Lord, I always want to hear from you because I know that you speak all the time. I want you to speak to me concerning my life, destiny, and purpose, Lord speaks to me in the name of Jesus.

5. I come against every power and principalities around me that won't make me hear from you, every environmental power, I destroy them by the fire of the holy ghost in the

name of Jesus. The scripture says once have you spoken, twice have I heard that all paper belongs to you. I pray that by your power, you will destroy every power and hindrance that is stopping me from hearing your voice crystal clear in the name of Jesus.

6. Lord Jesus, I want you to pour your spirit upon me. Your spirit that will give me the mental and spiritual alertness, I pray that you give it to me in the name of Jesus. Lord Jesus, unlock my spiritual ear today in the name of Jesus.

7. Father, thank You for the Blood of Jesus that gives us access into the Holy of Holies. Thank You for the power of the Spirit that strengthens us to do Your Will. To You alone be all the Glory, Lord in Jesus' Name.

8. Father, I ask in this season of Recovery, for an encounter with Your Presence that will restore every lost spiritual fire and passion in my life in

the Name of Jesus Christ. I ask for the recovery, restoration and impartation of spiritual fire and passion in my life, the church and our Nation, Lord in Jesus' Name.

9. Father, I ask in this season of Recovery, for an encounter with Your Presence that will restore every lost spiritual vision and direction in my life in Jesus' Name. I ask for the impartation, restoration and recovery of lost spiritual vision and direction in my life, the church and our Nation, Lord in Jesus' Name.

10. Father, in this season of Recovery, I ask for the restoration of Your tangible, feelable, palpable Presence and glory in my life. I ask for the recovery, restoration and impartation of Your Presence and glory in my life, the church, and our Nation, Lord in Jesus' Name.

11. Father, in this season of Recovery,

I ask for the impartation and restoration of boldness and confidence to face the future without fear. I reject the spirit of fear and timidity, inferiority and low self- worth in Jesus' Name.

Ask them to baptize you and teach you the ways of Christ.

Or contact us if you need guideline.

About the Author

Bishop Dr. Joseph C. Kanu has a medical background but was called by God to serve Him drastically through several visions, dreams, Prophecies and Confirmations.

He resisted God's calling for as long as he could but had to surrender to God's will in 2012 in London United Kingdom when God allowed every other door in life to become shut but left the door to God's house open to him.

He attended Bible School in London United Kingdom. He has an honorary doctorate for his accomplishments in God's kingdom. He also holds the title: Defender of the faith and other titles. He was set apart as a Bishop Elect and later consecrated into the office of a Bishop by the College of Bishops in London United Kingdom.

He is a Song Writer, Singer and Worshipper. He has written and produced his own songs and albums such as: Reggae Praise Medley, Redemption blood, Worship Medley Experience, The Man of Galilee, Praise Experience Medley, Your name is Rapha and Don't give up on Jesus (Rap Song).

He is also an intercessor and has produced
My prayer and prophecies for you (Audio).

He has also written several other books. Such as:

- Making room for your miracles. (Lessons from the Shunamite)

- How to hear from God everyday

- The Unfamiliar Touch

(Lesson from the woman with the issue of blood) to mention but a few.

- Living everyday under open heavens
  (lessons from Jacob's life)

- The Ministerial offices
  (Ethics and Etiquettes)

- Prayers That Availeth much

- Passover and Pentecost
(Their Power and Purpose)

He was ordained as an Evangelist in London and later on as a Pastor In Assemblies of God Church. He has served and trained as a minister in different churches such as RCCG, AG, BLW CFAN to mention but a few.

He was personally trained and imparted by the Late Evangelist Reinhard Bonke and his team when he was a student of his school of Evangelism in London.

He also received impartation and teaching from Benny Hinn, and late Morris Cerrulo to mention but a few

He runs School of Supernatural Ministry in London where he teaches and equips ministers to move in the Supernatural.

He is the presiding Bishop of Rapha Christian Centre house of Healing London. He travels the world with the message of God's kingdom, demonstrating the power of God in the Prophetic, Healing, Miraculous and Deliverance Ministries.

He is married to a British Citizen from South America/ Carribean Island Of Barbados and they are blessed with children.

Contact Details

Bishop Dr. Joseph C. Kanu

Presiding Bishop Rapha Christian Centre house of Healing London

And President of Bishop Joseph Global Ministries

36 Pitlake Croydon

London United Kingdom

Cr0 3RA

+4478 31 62 52 42

Email: Bishopjosephkanu@gmail.com

www.ingramcontent.com/pod-product-compliance
Lightning Source LLC
Chambersburg PA
CBHW020000050426
42450CB00005B/262